50 Satisfy Your Sweet Tooth Recipes for Home

By: Kelly Johnson

Table of Contents

- Chocolate Fudge Brownies
- Classic Vanilla Cupcakes
- Salted Caramel Cheesecake
- Lemon Meringue Pie
- Peanut Butter Chocolate Cookies
- Red Velvet Cake
- Cinnamon Sugar Donuts
- Raspberry Swirl Cheesecake Bars
- Triple Chocolate Mousse
- Blueberry Crumble
- Marshmallow Fudge Squares
- Butterscotch Pudding
- Strawberry Shortcake
- Maple Pecan Pie
- Oreo Stuffed Brownies
- Chocolate Chip Blondies
- Coconut Macaroons
- Almond Butter Brownies
- Classic Tiramisu
- Chocolate Eclairs
- Banana Cream Pie
- Pumpkin Spice Cupcakes
- Chocolate Peanut Butter Pie
- Key Lime Pie Bars
- Pistachio Ice Cream Sandwiches
- Cinnamon Roll Cake
- Dark Chocolate Truffles
- Cherry Cheesecake Bites
- Snickerdoodle Cookies
- Lemon Bars with Shortbread Crust
- Mocha Fudge Cake
- Nutella Swirled Brownies
- Apple Cinnamon Muffins
- Caramel Apple Tart
- Double Chocolate Chip Cookies

- Espresso Brownie Bites
- Honey Lavender Ice Cream
- Vanilla Bean Panna Cotta
- Strawberry Rhubarb Crumble
- Caramelized Banana Bread
- Chocolate Lava Cake
- Churro Bites with Chocolate Sauce
- Raspberry Lemon Bars
- Chocolate-Covered Marshmallow Pops
- Pineapple Upside-Down Cake
- Almond Joy Fudge
- Chocolate Hazelnut Tart
- Maple Bacon Cupcakes
- White Chocolate Raspberry Truffles
- Carrot Cake with Cream Cheese Frosting

Chocolate Fudge Brownies

Ingredients:

- 1 cup (225g) unsalted butter
- 8 oz (225g) semi-sweet chocolate, chopped
- 1 1/2 cups (300g) granulated sugar
- 4 large eggs
- 1 tsp vanilla extract
- 1 cup (125g) all-purpose flour
- 1/4 cup (30g) unsweetened cocoa powder
- 1/2 tsp salt
- 1 cup (175g) semi-sweet chocolate chips (optional)

Instructions:

1. **Preheat oven**: Set your oven to 350°F (175°C) and line a 9x13-inch baking pan with parchment paper.
2. **Melt butter and chocolate**: In a microwave-safe bowl, melt the butter and chopped chocolate in 30-second intervals, stirring in between until smooth. Let cool slightly.
3. **Mix sugar and eggs**: In a large mixing bowl, whisk together the sugar and eggs until combined. Stir in the vanilla extract.
4. **Combine wet and dry ingredients**: Slowly add the melted chocolate mixture to the sugar mixture and stir until well combined.
5. **Add dry ingredients**: Sift the flour, cocoa powder, and salt together. Gradually fold them into the wet mixture until just combined (don't overmix). Stir in the chocolate chips, if using.
6. **Bake**: Pour the batter into the prepared baking pan and spread evenly. Bake for 25-30 minutes, or until a toothpick inserted comes out with moist crumbs (not wet batter).
7. **Cool and serve**: Let the brownies cool in the pan before cutting into squares. Enjoy your rich, fudgy brownies!

Classic Vanilla Cupcakes

Ingredients:

- 1 1/2 cups (190g) all-purpose flour
- 1 1/2 tsp baking powder
- 1/4 tsp salt
- 1/2 cup (115g) unsalted butter, softened
- 1 cup (200g) granulated sugar
- 2 large eggs
- 2 tsp vanilla extract
- 1/2 cup (120ml) whole milk

Instructions:

1. **Preheat oven**: Preheat your oven to 350°F (175°C) and line a 12-cup muffin pan with cupcake liners.
2. **Mix dry ingredients**: In a medium bowl, whisk together the flour, baking powder, and salt.
3. **Cream butter and sugar**: In a large bowl, cream the butter and sugar until light and fluffy. Add the eggs one at a time, beating well after each addition. Stir in the vanilla extract.
4. **Combine wet and dry**: Gradually add the dry ingredients to the butter mixture, alternating with the milk, beginning and ending with the dry ingredients. Mix until just combined.
5. **Bake**: Divide the batter evenly among the cupcake liners and bake for 18-20 minutes, or until a toothpick inserted in the center comes out clean.
6. **Cool and frost**: Let the cupcakes cool completely before frosting with your favorite frosting.

Salted Caramel Cheesecake

Ingredients:

Crust:

- 1 1/2 cups (150g) graham cracker crumbs
- 1/4 cup (50g) granulated sugar
- 1/2 cup (115g) unsalted butter, melted

Cheesecake Filling:

- 24 oz (680g) cream cheese, softened
- 1 cup (200g) granulated sugar
- 1/2 cup (120ml) sour cream
- 2 tsp vanilla extract
- 3 large eggs

Salted Caramel Sauce:

- 1 cup (200g) granulated sugar
- 6 tbsp (90g) unsalted butter
- 1/2 cup (120ml) heavy cream
- 1 tsp sea salt

Instructions:

1. **Preheat oven and prepare crust**: Preheat the oven to 325°F (160°C). Mix the graham cracker crumbs, sugar, and melted butter together and press the mixture into the bottom of a 9-inch springform pan. Bake for 10 minutes and set aside.
2. **Make cheesecake filling**: Beat the cream cheese and sugar together until smooth and creamy. Add the sour cream and vanilla extract, mixing until combined. Add the eggs one at a time, beating just until incorporated.
3. **Bake**: Pour the cheesecake filling over the crust and bake for 50-60 minutes, or until the center is slightly jiggly but set around the edges. Turn off the oven, crack the door, and let the cheesecake cool inside for an hour before chilling in the refrigerator for at least 4 hours or overnight.
4. **Prepare salted caramel sauce**: Heat the sugar in a saucepan over medium heat, stirring constantly until it melts into a smooth amber liquid. Stir in the butter, then carefully pour in the heavy cream, continuing to stir. Boil for 1 minute, remove from heat, and stir in the salt. Let it cool.

5. **Serve**: Drizzle the cooled salted caramel sauce over the cheesecake before serving.

Lemon Meringue Pie

Ingredients:

Crust:

- 1 1/4 cups (160g) all-purpose flour
- 1/2 cup (115g) unsalted butter, cold and cubed
- 1/4 cup (60ml) ice water

Lemon Filling:

- 1 1/4 cups (250g) granulated sugar
- 1/2 cup (65g) cornstarch
- 1 1/2 cups (360ml) water
- 4 large egg yolks
- 2/3 cup (160ml) fresh lemon juice
- 2 tbsp lemon zest
- 2 tbsp unsalted butter

Meringue:

- 4 large egg whites
- 1/2 cup (100g) granulated sugar
- 1/4 tsp cream of tartar

Instructions:

1. **Prepare the crust**: In a food processor, pulse the flour and butter until the mixture resembles coarse crumbs. Slowly add the ice water and pulse until the dough comes together. Form into a disc, wrap in plastic, and chill for 30 minutes. Roll out the dough and fit it into a 9-inch pie pan. Bake at 375°F (190°C) for 15-20 minutes or until golden brown. Set aside to cool.
2. **Make the lemon filling**: In a medium saucepan, whisk together the sugar and cornstarch. Gradually stir in the water, cooking over medium heat until thickened. Whisk the egg yolks in a separate bowl, then slowly add the hot mixture to the yolks while whisking constantly. Return the mixture to the saucepan, cook for 2 more minutes, then stir in the lemon juice, zest, and butter. Pour into the baked crust.
3. **Make the meringue**: Beat the egg whites with cream of tartar until soft peaks form. Gradually add sugar, beating until stiff peaks form.

4. **Bake the pie**: Spread the meringue over the lemon filling, sealing it to the edges of the crust. Bake at 350°F (175°C) for 10-12 minutes or until the meringue is golden brown.
5. **Cool and serve**: Let the pie cool to room temperature before slicing and serving.

Peanut Butter Chocolate Cookies

Ingredients:

- 1 cup (240g) creamy peanut butter
- 1 cup (200g) granulated sugar
- 1 large egg
- 1 tsp vanilla extract
- 1/2 tsp baking soda
- 1/4 tsp salt
- 1 cup (175g) chocolate chips

Instructions:

1. **Preheat oven**: Preheat your oven to 350°F (175°C) and line a baking sheet with parchment paper.
2. **Mix ingredients**: In a large bowl, combine the peanut butter, sugar, egg, vanilla extract, baking soda, and salt. Mix until smooth.
3. **Add chocolate chips**: Fold in the chocolate chips until evenly distributed.
4. **Shape cookies**: Drop tablespoon-sized portions of dough onto the prepared baking sheet, spacing them about 2 inches apart.
5. **Bake**: Bake for 10-12 minutes, or until the edges are lightly golden. Let cool on the baking sheet for a few minutes before transferring to a wire rack to cool completely.

Red Velvet Cake

Ingredients:

For the Cake:

- 2 1/2 cups (315g) all-purpose flour
- 1 1/2 cups (300g) granulated sugar
- 1 tsp baking soda
- 1 tsp salt
- 1 tsp cocoa powder
- 1 1/2 cups (360ml) vegetable oil
- 1 cup (240ml) buttermilk, room temperature
- 2 large eggs
- 2 tbsp red food coloring
- 1 tsp vanilla extract
- 1 tsp white vinegar

For the Cream Cheese Frosting:

- 8 oz (225g) cream cheese, softened
- 1/2 cup (115g) unsalted butter, softened
- 4 cups (480g) powdered sugar
- 1 tsp vanilla extract

Instructions:

1. **Preheat oven**: Preheat your oven to 350°F (175°C). Grease and flour two 9-inch round cake pans.
2. **Mix dry ingredients**: In a large bowl, sift together the flour, sugar, baking soda, salt, and cocoa powder.
3. **Combine wet ingredients**: In another bowl, whisk together the oil, buttermilk, eggs, food coloring, vanilla extract, and vinegar.
4. **Combine wet and dry**: Gradually add the wet ingredients to the dry ingredients, mixing until just combined.
5. **Bake**: Divide the batter evenly between the prepared cake pans and bake for 25-30 minutes, or until a toothpick inserted in the center comes out clean. Let the cakes cool in the pans for 10 minutes before transferring to wire racks to cool completely.
6. **Make the frosting**: In a medium bowl, beat together the cream cheese and butter until smooth. Gradually add the powdered sugar and vanilla, mixing until creamy.

7. **Assemble the cake**: Frost the top of one cake layer, place the second layer on top, and frost the top and sides of the cake.

Cinnamon Sugar Donuts

Ingredients:

- 1 1/2 cups (190g) all-purpose flour
- 1/2 cup (100g) granulated sugar
- 2 tsp baking powder
- 1/2 tsp salt
- 1/2 tsp ground cinnamon
- 1/2 cup (120ml) milk
- 1 large egg
- 1/4 cup (60ml) vegetable oil
- 1/2 cup (100g) granulated sugar (for coating)
- 1 tsp ground cinnamon (for coating)

Instructions:

1. **Preheat oven**: Preheat your oven to 350°F (175°C) and grease a donut pan.
2. **Mix dry ingredients**: In a large bowl, whisk together the flour, sugar, baking powder, salt, and cinnamon.
3. **Combine wet ingredients**: In another bowl, mix together the milk, egg, and vegetable oil.
4. **Combine wet and dry**: Pour the wet ingredients into the dry ingredients and mix until just combined.
5. **Fill the donut pan**: Spoon the batter into the prepared donut pan, filling each cavity about 2/3 full.
6. **Bake**: Bake for 10-12 minutes, or until golden brown. Let cool in the pan for a few minutes before transferring to a wire rack.
7. **Coat in cinnamon sugar**: In a small bowl, combine the sugar and cinnamon. While the donuts are still warm, roll them in the cinnamon sugar mixture.

Raspberry Swirl Cheesecake Bars

Ingredients:

For the Crust:

- 1 cup (125g) graham cracker crumbs
- 1/4 cup (50g) granulated sugar
- 1/2 cup (115g) unsalted butter, melted

For the Cheesecake Filling:

- 16 oz (450g) cream cheese, softened
- 1 cup (200g) granulated sugar
- 2 large eggs
- 1 tsp vanilla extract
- 1 cup (240ml) sour cream

For the Raspberry Swirl:

- 1 cup (120g) fresh or frozen raspberries
- 2 tbsp granulated sugar
- 1 tbsp lemon juice

Instructions:

1. **Preheat oven**: Preheat your oven to 325°F (160°C) and line an 8x8-inch baking pan with parchment paper.
2. **Make the crust**: In a medium bowl, combine the graham cracker crumbs, sugar, and melted butter. Press the mixture into the bottom of the prepared pan. Bake for 10 minutes and let cool.
3. **Make the filling**: In a large bowl, beat together the cream cheese and sugar until smooth. Add the eggs one at a time, mixing well after each addition. Stir in the vanilla and sour cream until combined.
4. **Make the raspberry swirl**: In a small saucepan over medium heat, combine the raspberries, sugar, and lemon juice. Cook until the raspberries break down and the mixture thickens, about 5-7 minutes. Let it cool slightly.
5. **Assemble**: Pour the cheesecake filling over the crust. Drop spoonfuls of the raspberry mixture on top and use a knife or skewer to swirl it into the filling.

6. **Bake**: Bake for 40-45 minutes, or until the edges are set but the center is slightly jiggly. Turn off the oven and let the cheesecake bars cool inside for 1 hour. Refrigerate for at least 4 hours before slicing.

Triple Chocolate Mousse

Ingredients:

- 4 oz (115g) dark chocolate, chopped
- 4 oz (115g) milk chocolate, chopped
- 4 oz (115g) white chocolate, chopped
- 1 cup (240ml) heavy cream
- 3 large eggs, separated
- 1/4 cup (50g) granulated sugar
- 1/4 tsp salt

Instructions:

1. **Melt chocolates**: Melt the dark, milk, and white chocolate in separate bowls over a double boiler or in the microwave. Allow to cool slightly.
2. **Whip cream**: In a large bowl, whip the heavy cream until soft peaks form. Set aside.
3. **Make chocolate mousses**: For each chocolate layer, in a separate bowl, beat the egg whites until soft peaks form, gradually adding the sugar until stiff peaks form. Gently fold in the melted chocolate into each bowl, then fold in the whipped cream until fully incorporated.
4. **Layer mousses**: In serving glasses, layer the dark chocolate mousse, followed by the milk chocolate mousse, and finally the white chocolate mousse.
5. **Chill**: Refrigerate for at least 2 hours before serving.

Blueberry Crumble

Ingredients:

For the Filling:

- 4 cups (600g) fresh or frozen blueberries
- 1/2 cup (100g) granulated sugar
- 1 tbsp lemon juice
- 1 tbsp cornstarch

For the Crumble Topping:

- 1 cup (125g) all-purpose flour
- 1/2 cup (50g) rolled oats
- 1/2 cup (100g) brown sugar
- 1/2 tsp cinnamon
- 1/4 cup (60g) unsalted butter, melted

Instructions:

1. **Preheat oven**: Preheat your oven to 350°F (175°C) and grease an 8x8-inch baking dish.
2. **Prepare the filling**: In a bowl, mix the blueberries with sugar, lemon juice, and cornstarch. Pour into the prepared baking dish.
3. **Make the crumble topping**: In another bowl, combine the flour, oats, brown sugar, and cinnamon. Stir in the melted butter until crumbly.
4. **Assemble and bake**: Sprinkle the crumble topping over the blueberry filling. Bake for 30-35 minutes, or until the topping is golden brown and the blueberries are bubbling.
5. **Cool and serve**: Allow to cool slightly before serving.

Marshmallow Fudge Squares

Ingredients:

- 2 cups (400g) granulated sugar
- 1/2 cup (120ml) evaporated milk
- 1/2 cup (115g) unsalted butter
- 2 cups (340g) semi-sweet chocolate chips
- 2 cups (200g) mini marshmallows
- 1 tsp vanilla extract
- 1/2 cup (80g) chopped nuts (optional)

Instructions:

1. **Prepare the pan**: Line an 8x8-inch baking pan with foil, leaving an overhang for easy removal.
2. **Make the fudge**: In a saucepan over medium heat, combine the sugar, evaporated milk, and butter. Stir until it reaches a boil and cook for 5 minutes, stirring constantly.
3. **Add chocolate**: Remove from heat and stir in the chocolate chips until melted and smooth. Mix in the marshmallows, vanilla extract, and nuts, if using.
4. **Transfer to pan**: Pour the fudge mixture into the prepared pan and spread evenly.
5. **Cool and cut**: Let cool completely at room temperature or in the refrigerator before cutting into squares.

Butterscotch Pudding

Ingredients:

- 1/2 cup (100g) packed brown sugar
- 2 tbsp cornstarch
- 1/4 tsp salt
- 2 cups (480ml) milk
- 3 tbsp unsalted butter
- 1 tsp vanilla extract

Instructions:

1. **Combine dry ingredients**: In a saucepan, whisk together the brown sugar, cornstarch, and salt.
2. **Add milk**: Gradually whisk in the milk until smooth.
3. **Cook the pudding**: Cook over medium heat, stirring constantly, until the mixture thickens and bubbles.
4. **Add butter and vanilla**: Remove from heat and stir in the butter and vanilla extract until smooth.
5. **Cool**: Pour the pudding into serving dishes and let cool for at least 30 minutes before serving.

Feel free to ask if you need any more adjustments!

Strawberry Shortcake

Ingredients:

For the Shortcake:

- 2 cups (250g) all-purpose flour
- 1/4 cup (50g) granulated sugar
- 1 tbsp baking powder
- 1/2 tsp salt
- 1/2 cup (115g) unsalted butter, cold and cubed
- 3/4 cup (180ml) heavy cream

For the Strawberries:

- 4 cups (600g) fresh strawberries, hulled and sliced
- 1/4 cup (50g) granulated sugar

For the Whipped Cream:

- 1 cup (240ml) heavy cream
- 2 tbsp powdered sugar
- 1 tsp vanilla extract

Instructions:

1. **Preheat oven**: Preheat your oven to 400°F (200°C). Grease and flour a baking sheet.
2. **Make the shortcake**: In a large bowl, mix the flour, sugar, baking powder, and salt. Cut in the butter until the mixture resembles coarse crumbs. Stir in the heavy cream until just combined.
3. **Shape and bake**: Turn the dough onto a floured surface, knead gently, and roll out to about 1-inch thick. Cut into rounds and place on the baking sheet. Bake for 15-20 minutes, or until golden.
4. **Prepare strawberries**: In a bowl, toss the sliced strawberries with sugar and let sit for about 30 minutes to release their juices.
5. **Make whipped cream**: In a medium bowl, beat the heavy cream, powdered sugar, and vanilla until soft peaks form.
6. **Assemble**: Split the shortcakes in half, spoon the strawberries and their juices on the bottom half, add whipped cream, and top with the other half.

Maple Pecan Pie

Ingredients:

- 1 unbaked 9-inch pie crust
- 1 cup (240ml) maple syrup
- 1 cup (200g) packed brown sugar
- 1/3 cup (80ml) unsalted butter, melted
- 3 large eggs
- 1 tsp vanilla extract
- 1 1/2 cups (150g) pecan halves

Instructions:

1. **Preheat oven**: Preheat your oven to 350°F (175°C).
2. **Prepare filling**: In a large bowl, whisk together the maple syrup, brown sugar, melted butter, eggs, and vanilla until smooth. Stir in the pecans.
3. **Fill pie crust**: Pour the filling into the unbaked pie crust.
4. **Bake**: Bake for 50-60 minutes, or until the filling is set and the crust is golden. Let cool before slicing.

Oreo Stuffed Brownies

Ingredients:

- 1 cup (225g) unsalted butter
- 2 cups (400g) granulated sugar
- 4 large eggs
- 1 tsp vanilla extract
- 1 cup (125g) all-purpose flour
- 1 cup (90g) unsweetened cocoa powder
- 1/2 tsp salt
- 1/2 tsp baking powder
- 16 Oreo cookies

Instructions:

1. **Preheat oven**: Preheat your oven to 350°F (175°C) and grease a 9x13-inch baking dish.
2. **Melt butter**: In a saucepan, melt the butter over medium heat. Remove from heat and stir in the sugar, eggs, and vanilla until smooth.
3. **Mix dry ingredients**: In a separate bowl, combine the flour, cocoa powder, salt, and baking powder. Gradually add to the butter mixture, mixing until just combined.
4. **Layer Oreos**: Pour half of the brownie batter into the prepared baking dish. Layer the Oreos on top, then pour the remaining batter over the Oreos.
5. **Bake**: Bake for 25-30 minutes or until a toothpick inserted in the center comes out with a few moist crumbs. Let cool before cutting into squares.

Chocolate Chip Blondies

Ingredients:

- 1/2 cup (115g) unsalted butter, melted
- 1 cup (200g) brown sugar
- 1/2 cup (100g) granulated sugar
- 2 large eggs
- 1 tsp vanilla extract
- 1 1/2 cups (190g) all-purpose flour
- 1/2 tsp baking powder
- 1/4 tsp salt
- 1 cup (175g) chocolate chips

Instructions:

1. **Preheat oven**: Preheat your oven to 350°F (175°C) and grease a 9x9-inch baking pan.
2. **Mix wet ingredients**: In a large bowl, combine the melted butter, brown sugar, and granulated sugar. Mix in the eggs and vanilla until well combined.
3. **Add dry ingredients**: Stir in the flour, baking powder, and salt until just combined. Fold in the chocolate chips.
4. **Bake**: Pour the batter into the prepared pan and spread evenly. Bake for 25-30 minutes or until a toothpick inserted comes out clean. Let cool before slicing.

Coconut Macaroons

Ingredients:

- 3 cups (240g) sweetened shredded coconut
- 1/2 cup (100g) granulated sugar
- 1/4 cup (30g) all-purpose flour
- 1/4 tsp salt
- 4 large egg whites
- 1 tsp vanilla extract
- 1/2 cup (90g) semi-sweet chocolate chips (optional)

Instructions:

1. **Preheat oven**: Preheat your oven to 325°F (160°C) and line a baking sheet with parchment paper.
2. **Mix ingredients**: In a large bowl, combine the coconut, sugar, flour, salt, egg whites, and vanilla extract until well mixed.
3. **Shape macaroons**: Use a small cookie scoop or your hands to form mounds of the mixture and place them on the prepared baking sheet.
4. **Bake**: Bake for 15-20 minutes, or until golden brown. Let cool.
5. **Optional chocolate dip**: If desired, melt chocolate chips and dip the bottoms of the macaroons into the chocolate. Let set on parchment paper.

Almond Butter Brownies

Ingredients:

- 1/2 cup (115g) unsalted butter, melted
- 1 cup (200g) granulated sugar
- 1/2 cup (120g) almond butter
- 2 large eggs
- 1 tsp vanilla extract
- 1/2 cup (65g) all-purpose flour
- 1/4 cup (30g) unsweetened cocoa powder
- 1/4 tsp salt

Instructions:

1. **Preheat oven**: Preheat your oven to 350°F (175°C) and grease an 8x8-inch baking pan.
2. **Mix wet ingredients**: In a large bowl, combine the melted butter, sugar, almond butter, eggs, and vanilla until smooth.
3. **Add dry ingredients**: Stir in the flour, cocoa powder, and salt until just combined.
4. **Bake**: Pour the batter into the prepared pan and spread evenly. Bake for 25-30 minutes or until a toothpick inserted comes out clean. Let cool before cutting.

Classic Tiramisu

Ingredients:

- 6 large egg yolks
- 3/4 cup (150g) granulated sugar
- 2/3 cup (160ml) milk
- 1 1/4 cups (300ml) heavy cream
- 1 cup (240ml) strong brewed coffee, cooled
- 2 tbsp coffee liqueur (optional)
- 24 ladyfinger cookies
- Unsweetened cocoa powder for dusting

Instructions:

1. **Prepare custard**: In a saucepan, whisk together the egg yolks and sugar. Add the milk and cook over low heat, stirring constantly until thickened. Remove from heat and let cool.
2. **Whip cream**: In a separate bowl, whip the heavy cream until stiff peaks form. Fold the whipped cream into the cooled custard mixture.
3. **Layer ingredients**: In a shallow dish, combine the coffee and coffee liqueur. Quickly dip each ladyfinger into the coffee mixture and layer them in a serving dish.
4. **Assemble**: Spread half of the custard over the ladyfingers, then add another layer of dipped ladyfingers followed by the remaining custard.
5. **Chill**: Cover and refrigerate for at least 4 hours or overnight. Dust with cocoa powder before serving.

Chocolate Eclairs

Ingredients:

For the Choux Pastry:

- 1 cup (240ml) water
- 1/2 cup (115g) unsalted butter
- 1 cup (125g) all-purpose flour
- 1/4 tsp salt
- 4 large eggs

For the Pastry Cream:

- 2 cups (480ml) milk
- 1/2 cup (100g) granulated sugar
- 1/4 cup (30g) cornstarch
- 4 large egg yolks
- 2 tbsp unsalted butter
- 1 tsp vanilla extract

For the Chocolate Glaze:

- 1/2 cup (90g) semi-sweet chocolate chips
- 2 tbsp unsalted butter

Instructions:

1. **Make choux pastry**: Preheat your oven to 400°F (200°C). In a saucepan, combine water and butter; bring to a boil. Remove from heat and stir in flour and salt until a dough forms. Let cool slightly, then add eggs one at a time until smooth.
2. **Pipe eclairs**: Transfer the dough to a piping bag and pipe 4-inch long strips onto a baking sheet lined with parchment paper. Bake for 20-25 minutes until golden and puffed. Let cool.
3. **Make pastry cream**: In a saucepan, heat milk until simmering. In a bowl, whisk together sugar, cornstarch, and egg yolks. Gradually whisk in hot milk. Return to heat and cook until thickened. Remove from heat, stir in butter and vanilla. Cool completely.
4. **Fill eclairs**: Once the choux pastries are cool, use a piping bag to fill each with pastry cream.

5. **Make glaze**: In a microwave-safe bowl, melt chocolate chips and butter together. Stir until smooth.
6. **Glaze eclairs**: Dip the tops of the filled eclairs into the chocolate glaze and let set before serving.

Feel free to ask if you need any more adjustments or additional recipes!

Banana Cream Pie

Ingredients:

For the Crust:

- 1 1/2 cups (150g) graham cracker crumbs
- 1/4 cup (50g) granulated sugar
- 1/2 cup (115g) unsalted butter, melted

For the Filling:

- 2 cups (480ml) whole milk
- 3/4 cup (150g) granulated sugar
- 1/3 cup (40g) cornstarch
- 1/4 tsp salt
- 3 large egg yolks
- 2 tbsp unsalted butter
- 1 tsp vanilla extract
- 3 ripe bananas, sliced

For the Whipped Cream:

- 1 cup (240ml) heavy cream
- 2 tbsp powdered sugar
- 1 tsp vanilla extract

Instructions:

1. **Preheat oven**: Preheat your oven to 350°F (175°C).
2. **Make crust**: In a bowl, combine graham cracker crumbs, sugar, and melted butter. Press into a 9-inch pie pan. Bake for 8-10 minutes until lightly browned. Let cool.
3. **Prepare filling**: In a saucepan, whisk together milk, sugar, cornstarch, and salt. Cook over medium heat, stirring until thickened. Whisk a small amount into the egg yolks, then return to the saucepan and cook for 2 more minutes. Stir in butter and vanilla.
4. **Layer bananas**: Place banana slices in the cooled crust, pour the filling over them, and let it cool to room temperature.
5. **Make whipped cream**: In a bowl, beat heavy cream, powdered sugar, and vanilla until soft peaks form.

6. **Top pie**: Spread whipped cream over the pie and refrigerate for at least 4 hours before serving.

Pumpkin Spice Cupcakes

Ingredients:

- 1 1/2 cups (190g) all-purpose flour
- 1 cup (200g) granulated sugar
- 1 tsp baking soda
- 1/2 tsp baking powder
- 1/2 tsp salt
- 1 tbsp pumpkin pie spice
- 1/2 cup (120ml) vegetable oil
- 1 cup (240ml) canned pumpkin puree
- 2 large eggs
- 1 tsp vanilla extract

Instructions:

1. **Preheat oven**: Preheat your oven to 350°F (175°C) and line a muffin tin with cupcake liners.
2. **Mix dry ingredients**: In a bowl, whisk together flour, sugar, baking soda, baking powder, salt, and pumpkin pie spice.
3. **Mix wet ingredients**: In another bowl, whisk together oil, pumpkin, eggs, and vanilla until smooth.
4. **Combine**: Add the wet ingredients to the dry ingredients and mix until just combined.
5. **Bake**: Divide the batter among the cupcake liners and bake for 18-20 minutes or until a toothpick inserted comes out clean. Let cool completely.

Chocolate Peanut Butter Pie

Ingredients:

For the Crust:

- 1 1/2 cups (150g) chocolate cookie crumbs
- 1/4 cup (50g) granulated sugar
- 1/2 cup (115g) unsalted butter, melted

For the Filling:

- 1 cup (240ml) heavy cream
- 1/2 cup (120ml) creamy peanut butter
- 1 cup (120g) powdered sugar
- 1 tsp vanilla extract

For the Topping:

- 1 cup (240ml) heavy cream
- 2 tbsp powdered sugar
- 1/2 cup (90g) chocolate chips

Instructions:

1. **Preheat oven**: Preheat your oven to 350°F (175°C).
2. **Make crust**: In a bowl, mix chocolate cookie crumbs, sugar, and melted butter. Press into a 9-inch pie pan and bake for 8-10 minutes. Let cool.
3. **Prepare filling**: In a bowl, whip heavy cream until stiff peaks form. In another bowl, mix peanut butter, powdered sugar, and vanilla until smooth. Fold in the whipped cream until combined.
4. **Fill crust**: Pour the filling into the cooled crust and smooth the top.
5. **Make topping**: In a bowl, whip heavy cream and powdered sugar until stiff peaks form. Spread over the filling.
6. **Chill**: Refrigerate for at least 4 hours before serving. Drizzle melted chocolate over the top if desired.

Key Lime Pie Bars

Ingredients:

For the Crust:

- 1 1/2 cups (190g) graham cracker crumbs
- 1/4 cup (50g) granulated sugar
- 1/2 cup (115g) unsalted butter, melted

For the Filling:

- 2 cans (14 oz each) sweetened condensed milk
- 1 cup (240ml) fresh key lime juice
- 4 large egg yolks
- Zest of 2 limes

Instructions:

1. **Preheat oven**: Preheat your oven to 350°F (175°C).
2. **Make crust**: In a bowl, combine graham cracker crumbs, sugar, and melted butter. Press into the bottom of a greased 9x13-inch baking dish. Bake for 10 minutes and let cool.
3. **Prepare filling**: In a bowl, whisk together sweetened condensed milk, key lime juice, egg yolks, and lime zest until smooth.
4. **Fill crust**: Pour the filling over the cooled crust.
5. **Bake**: Bake for 20-25 minutes or until set. Let cool at room temperature, then refrigerate for at least 2 hours before cutting into bars.

Pistachio Ice Cream Sandwiches

Ingredients:

For the Cookies:

- 1 cup (225g) unsalted butter, softened
- 1 cup (200g) granulated sugar
- 1 cup (220g) packed brown sugar
- 2 large eggs
- 2 tsp vanilla extract
- 3 cups (375g) all-purpose flour
- 1 tsp baking soda
- 1/2 tsp salt
- 1 cup (150g) chopped pistachios

For the Ice Cream:

- 2 cups (480ml) pistachio ice cream, softened

Instructions:

1. **Preheat oven**: Preheat your oven to 350°F (175°C).
2. **Make cookie dough**: In a large bowl, cream together butter, granulated sugar, and brown sugar until fluffy. Beat in eggs and vanilla. In another bowl, mix flour, baking soda, and salt. Gradually add to the creamed mixture. Stir in chopped pistachios.
3. **Bake cookies**: Drop spoonfuls of dough onto baking sheets and bake for 10-12 minutes until lightly golden. Let cool completely.
4. **Assemble sandwiches**: Place a scoop of pistachio ice cream between two cookies and press together. Freeze for 30 minutes before serving.

Cinnamon Roll Cake

Ingredients:

For the Cake:

- 2 cups (250g) all-purpose flour
- 1 tbsp baking powder
- 1/2 tsp salt
- 1 cup (200g) granulated sugar
- 1/2 cup (115g) unsalted butter, softened
- 1 large egg
- 1 tsp vanilla extract
- 1 cup (240ml) milk

For the Cinnamon Swirl:

- 1/2 cup (100g) packed brown sugar
- 1 tbsp ground cinnamon
- 1/4 cup (60g) unsalted butter, melted

For the Glaze:

- 1 cup (120g) powdered sugar
- 2-3 tbsp milk
- 1/2 tsp vanilla extract

Instructions:

1. **Preheat oven**: Preheat your oven to 350°F (175°C) and grease a 9x13-inch baking dish.
2. **Make batter**: In a bowl, mix flour, baking powder, and salt. In another bowl, cream together sugar and butter. Add egg and vanilla, then milk, alternating with the dry ingredients.
3. **Prepare swirl**: In a small bowl, combine brown sugar and cinnamon. Stir in melted butter.
4. **Layer cake**: Pour half of the batter into the prepared baking dish. Sprinkle with cinnamon mixture, then top with remaining batter.
5. **Bake**: Bake for 30-35 minutes or until a toothpick comes out clean.
6. **Make glaze**: In a bowl, mix powdered sugar, milk, and vanilla until smooth. Drizzle over cooled cake before serving.

Dark Chocolate Truffles

Ingredients:

- 8 oz (225g) dark chocolate, chopped
- 1/2 cup (120ml) heavy cream
- 1 tsp vanilla extract
- Cocoa powder or chopped nuts for rolling

Instructions:

1. **Heat cream**: In a saucepan, heat the heavy cream until simmering.
2. **Melt chocolate**: Pour the hot cream over the chopped chocolate and let sit for a minute. Stir until smooth. Add vanilla extract and mix well.
3. **Chill mixture**: Refrigerate for 1-2 hours until firm.
4. **Form truffles**: Using a small scoop or spoon, form the mixture into small balls and roll in cocoa powder or chopped nuts.
5. **Serve**: Store in the refrigerator until ready to serve.

Cherry Cheesecake Bites

Ingredients:

For the Crust:

- 1 cup (150g) graham cracker crumbs
- 1/4 cup (50g) granulated sugar
- 1/2 cup (115g) unsalted butter, melted

For the Filling:

- 8 oz (225g) cream cheese, softened
- 1/2 cup (100g) granulated sugar
- 1 tsp vanilla extract
- 1 large egg
- 1 cup (240ml) cherry pie filling

Instructions:

1. **Preheat oven**: Preheat your oven to 350°F (175°C). Line a mini muffin tin with paper liners.
2. **Make crust**: In a bowl, combine graham cracker crumbs, sugar, and melted butter. Press into the bottom of each liner.
3. **Prepare filling**: In another bowl, beat together cream cheese, sugar, vanilla, and egg until smooth.
4. **Fill crusts**: Pour the filling over the crusts, filling each cup about 3/4 full.
5. **Top with cherries**: Spoon a small amount of cherry pie filling on top of each bite.
6. **Bake**: Bake for 15-18 minutes or until set. Let cool completely before serving.

Feel free to ask if you need more recipes or adjustments!

Snickerdoodle Cookies

Ingredients:

- 1 cup (225g) unsalted butter, softened
- 1 1/2 cups (300g) granulated sugar
- 2 large eggs
- 2 3/4 cups (340g) all-purpose flour
- 2 tsp cream of tartar
- 1 tsp baking soda
- 1/2 tsp salt
- 1/4 cup (50g) granulated sugar (for rolling)
- 2 tsp ground cinnamon (for rolling)

Instructions:

1. **Preheat oven**: Preheat your oven to 350°F (175°C).
2. **Cream butter and sugar**: In a large bowl, beat together the butter and 1 1/2 cups sugar until light and fluffy. Add eggs one at a time, mixing well after each addition.
3. **Mix dry ingredients**: In another bowl, whisk together flour, cream of tartar, baking soda, and salt. Gradually add to the butter mixture until just combined.
4. **Prepare cinnamon sugar**: In a small bowl, mix together 1/4 cup sugar and cinnamon.
5. **Form cookies**: Roll dough into 1-inch balls, then roll in the cinnamon sugar mixture. Place on ungreased baking sheets.
6. **Bake**: Bake for 8-10 minutes or until the edges are set. Let cool on the baking sheet for a few minutes before transferring to a wire rack.

Lemon Bars with Shortbread Crust

Ingredients:

For the Crust:

- 1 cup (225g) unsalted butter, softened
- 1/2 cup (50g) powdered sugar
- 2 cups (250g) all-purpose flour
- 1/4 tsp salt

For the Filling:

- 1 cup (200g) granulated sugar
- 2 large eggs
- 1/2 cup (120ml) freshly squeezed lemon juice
- Zest of 2 lemons
- 1/4 cup (30g) all-purpose flour
- Powdered sugar for dusting

Instructions:

1. **Preheat oven**: Preheat your oven to 350°F (175°C) and grease a 9x13-inch baking dish.
2. **Make crust**: In a bowl, cream together the butter and powdered sugar. Gradually add flour and salt, mixing until crumbly. Press into the bottom of the prepared baking dish.
3. **Bake crust**: Bake for 15-20 minutes until lightly golden.
4. **Prepare filling**: In another bowl, whisk together granulated sugar, eggs, lemon juice, lemon zest, and flour until smooth.
5. **Fill crust**: Pour the filling over the baked crust.
6. **Bake**: Bake for an additional 20-25 minutes or until the filling is set. Let cool completely before dusting with powdered sugar and cutting into squares.

Mocha Fudge Cake

Ingredients:

For the Cake:

- 1 cup (240ml) brewed coffee, cooled
- 1/2 cup (120ml) vegetable oil
- 1 cup (200g) granulated sugar
- 1 cup (220g) packed brown sugar
- 2 large eggs
- 1 tsp vanilla extract
- 1 3/4 cups (220g) all-purpose flour
- 1/2 cup (50g) unsweetened cocoa powder
- 1 1/2 tsp baking powder
- 1/2 tsp baking soda
- 1/4 tsp salt

For the Frosting:

- 1/2 cup (115g) unsalted butter, softened
- 1/2 cup (50g) unsweetened cocoa powder
- 2 cups (240g) powdered sugar
- 1/4 cup (60ml) brewed coffee

Instructions:

1. **Preheat oven**: Preheat your oven to 350°F (175°C). Grease and flour two 9-inch round cake pans.
2. **Mix wet ingredients**: In a large bowl, combine coffee, oil, granulated sugar, brown sugar, eggs, and vanilla. Mix well.
3. **Combine dry ingredients**: In another bowl, whisk together flour, cocoa powder, baking powder, baking soda, and salt. Gradually add to the wet ingredients, mixing until combined.
4. **Bake**: Divide the batter between the prepared pans and bake for 25-30 minutes or until a toothpick comes out clean. Let cool completely.
5. **Make frosting**: In a bowl, beat butter and cocoa until smooth. Gradually add powdered sugar and coffee, beating until creamy.
6. **Frost cake**: Once the cake layers are cool, frost the top of one layer, place the second layer on top, and frost the top and sides.

Nutella Swirled Brownies

Ingredients:

- 1/2 cup (115g) unsalted butter
- 1 cup (200g) granulated sugar
- 2 large eggs
- 1 tsp vanilla extract
- 1/3 cup (40g) unsweetened cocoa powder
- 1 cup (125g) all-purpose flour
- 1/4 tsp salt
- 1/4 tsp baking powder
- 1/2 cup (150g) Nutella

Instructions:

1. **Preheat oven**: Preheat your oven to 350°F (175°C) and grease an 8x8-inch baking pan.
2. **Melt butter**: In a saucepan, melt butter over low heat. Remove from heat and stir in sugar, eggs, and vanilla.
3. **Mix dry ingredients**: In a separate bowl, whisk together cocoa powder, flour, salt, and baking powder. Gradually add to the wet mixture, stirring until combined.
4. **Spread batter**: Pour half the brownie batter into the prepared pan. Drop spoonfuls of Nutella over the batter and swirl with a knife. Pour remaining batter on top and swirl again.
5. **Bake**: Bake for 20-25 minutes or until a toothpick comes out with a few moist crumbs. Let cool before cutting into squares.

Apple Cinnamon Muffins

Ingredients:

- 2 cups (250g) all-purpose flour
- 1/2 cup (100g) granulated sugar
- 1/2 cup (120ml) vegetable oil
- 1 cup (240ml) milk
- 2 large eggs
- 1 tbsp baking powder
- 1/2 tsp salt
- 1 tsp ground cinnamon
- 2 cups (300g) diced apples

Instructions:

1. **Preheat oven**: Preheat your oven to 375°F (190°C) and line a muffin tin with paper liners.
2. **Mix wet ingredients**: In a large bowl, whisk together oil, milk, and eggs.
3. **Combine dry ingredients**: In another bowl, mix flour, sugar, baking powder, salt, and cinnamon. Gradually add to the wet mixture, stirring until just combined.
4. **Fold in apples**: Gently fold in diced apples.
5. **Bake**: Divide the batter among muffin cups and bake for 20-25 minutes or until a toothpick comes out clean. Let cool before serving.

Caramel Apple Tart

Ingredients:

For the Tart Crust:

- 1 1/2 cups (190g) all-purpose flour
- 1/2 cup (100g) powdered sugar
- 1/2 cup (115g) unsalted butter, softened
- 1/4 tsp salt

For the Filling:

- 4 cups (600g) sliced apples (about 4 medium apples)
- 1/2 cup (100g) granulated sugar
- 1 tsp ground cinnamon
- 1/4 cup (60ml) caramel sauce

Instructions:

1. **Preheat oven**: Preheat your oven to 350°F (175°C). Grease a tart pan.
2. **Make crust**: In a bowl, mix flour, powdered sugar, butter, and salt until crumbly. Press into the bottom and up the sides of the tart pan.
3. **Bake crust**: Bake for 15-20 minutes or until lightly golden.
4. **Prepare filling**: In a bowl, toss sliced apples with sugar and cinnamon.
5. **Assemble tart**: Arrange apple slices over the baked crust. Drizzle with caramel sauce.
6. **Bake**: Bake for an additional 25-30 minutes or until apples are tender. Let cool before serving.

Double Chocolate Chip Cookies

Ingredients:

- 1/2 cup (115g) unsalted butter, softened
- 1/2 cup (100g) granulated sugar
- 1/2 cup (100g) packed brown sugar
- 1 large egg
- 1 tsp vanilla extract
- 1 cup (125g) all-purpose flour
- 1/3 cup (40g) unsweetened cocoa powder
- 1/2 tsp baking soda
- 1/4 tsp salt
- 1 cup (175g) chocolate chips

Instructions:

1. **Preheat oven**: Preheat your oven to 350°F (175°C) and line a baking sheet with parchment paper.
2. **Cream butter and sugars**: In a bowl, cream together butter, granulated sugar, and brown sugar. Add egg and vanilla, mixing until combined.
3. **Combine dry ingredients**: In another bowl, whisk together flour, cocoa powder, baking soda, and salt. Gradually add to the wet mixture.
4. **Add chocolate chips**: Fold in chocolate chips.
5. **Drop dough**: Drop spoonfuls of dough onto the prepared baking sheet.
6. **Bake**: Bake for 10-12 minutes or until edges are set. Let cool before transferring to a wire rack.

Espresso Brownie Bites

Ingredients:

- 1/2 cup (115g) unsalted butter
- 1 cup (200g) granulated sugar
- 2 large eggs
- 1 tsp vanilla extract
- 1/3 cup (40g) unsweetened cocoa powder
- 1/2 cup (65g) all-purpose flour
- 1/4 tsp salt
- 1 tbsp instant espresso powder
- 1/2 cup (90g) chocolate chips

Instructions:

1. **Preheat oven**: Preheat your oven to 350°F (175°C) and grease a mini muffin tin.
2. **Melt butter**: In a saucepan, melt butter over low heat. Remove from heat and stir in sugar, eggs, and vanilla.
3. **Mix dry ingredients**: In a separate bowl, whisk together cocoa powder, flour, salt, and espresso powder. Gradually add to the wet mixture, stirring until combined.
4. **Add chocolate chips**: Fold in chocolate chips.
5. **Fill muffin tin**: Pour batter into the mini muffin tin, filling each cup about 2/3 full.
6. **Bake**: Bake for 10-12 minutes or until a toothpick comes out with a few moist crumbs. Let cool before serving.

Feel free to ask for more recipes or any adjustments!

Honey Lavender Ice Cream

Ingredients:

- 2 cups (480ml) heavy cream
- 1 cup (240ml) whole milk
- 3/4 cup (150g) granulated sugar
- 1/4 cup (60ml) honey
- 1 tbsp dried culinary lavender
- 1 tsp vanilla extract
- Pinch of salt

Instructions:

1. **Infuse the cream**: In a saucepan, combine heavy cream, milk, sugar, honey, and lavender. Heat over medium until sugar dissolves, then remove from heat and let steep for 30 minutes.
2. **Strain mixture**: Strain the mixture through a fine mesh sieve to remove lavender.
3. **Add vanilla and salt**: Stir in vanilla extract and a pinch of salt.
4. **Chill**: Refrigerate the mixture for at least 4 hours or overnight.
5. **Churn**: Churn in an ice cream maker according to manufacturer's instructions. Transfer to a container and freeze until firm.

Vanilla Bean Panna Cotta

Ingredients:

- 2 cups (480ml) heavy cream
- 1/2 cup (100g) granulated sugar
- 1 tsp vanilla bean paste or 1 vanilla bean, split and seeds scraped
- 1 packet (2 1/4 tsp) unflavored gelatin
- 3 tbsp cold water

Instructions:

1. **Heat cream and sugar**: In a saucepan, combine heavy cream, sugar, and vanilla. Heat over medium until sugar dissolves, then remove from heat.
2. **Bloom gelatin**: In a small bowl, sprinkle gelatin over cold water and let sit for 5 minutes.
3. **Combine**: Stir bloomed gelatin into the warm cream mixture until dissolved.
4. **Pour into molds**: Pour into serving cups or molds and refrigerate for at least 4 hours until set.
5. **Serve**: To serve, unmold onto plates or enjoy in the cups.

Strawberry Rhubarb Crumble

Ingredients:

For the Filling:

- 2 cups (300g) sliced strawberries
- 2 cups (300g) sliced rhubarb
- 1 cup (200g) granulated sugar
- 1 tbsp cornstarch
- 1 tbsp lemon juice

For the Crumble:

- 1 cup (125g) all-purpose flour
- 1/2 cup (100g) brown sugar
- 1/2 cup (45g) rolled oats
- 1/4 cup (60g) unsalted butter, softened
- 1/4 tsp salt

Instructions:

1. **Preheat oven**: Preheat your oven to 350°F (175°C).
2. **Prepare filling**: In a bowl, combine strawberries, rhubarb, sugar, cornstarch, and lemon juice. Pour into a greased baking dish.
3. **Make crumble**: In another bowl, mix flour, brown sugar, oats, butter, and salt until crumbly.
4. **Top filling**: Sprinkle the crumble mixture over the fruit filling.
5. **Bake**: Bake for 30-35 minutes or until the filling is bubbling and the topping is golden. Let cool before serving.

Caramelized Banana Bread

Ingredients:

- 3 ripe bananas, mashed
- 1/2 cup (115g) unsalted butter, melted
- 1 cup (200g) granulated sugar
- 2 large eggs
- 1 tsp vanilla extract
- 1 1/2 cups (190g) all-purpose flour
- 1 tsp baking soda
- 1/4 tsp salt
- 1/2 cup (80g) chopped walnuts (optional)

Instructions:

1. **Preheat oven**: Preheat your oven to 350°F (175°C) and grease a loaf pan.
2. **Mix wet ingredients**: In a bowl, mix mashed bananas, melted butter, sugar, eggs, and vanilla.
3. **Combine dry ingredients**: In another bowl, whisk together flour, baking soda, and salt. Gradually add to the wet mixture.
4. **Add walnuts**: Fold in chopped walnuts if using.
5. **Bake**: Pour batter into the prepared loaf pan and bake for 60-70 minutes or until a toothpick comes out clean. Let cool before slicing.

Chocolate Lava Cake

Ingredients:

- 1/2 cup (115g) unsalted butter
- 1 cup (170g) semi-sweet chocolate chips
- 2 large eggs
- 2 large egg yolks
- 1/4 cup (50g) granulated sugar
- 2 tbsp all-purpose flour
- 1/4 tsp salt

Instructions:

1. **Preheat oven**: Preheat your oven to 425°F (220°C) and grease four ramekins.
2. **Melt chocolate and butter**: In a microwave-safe bowl, melt butter and chocolate chips together until smooth.
3. **Mix eggs and sugar**: In another bowl, whisk eggs, egg yolks, and sugar until thick and pale.
4. **Combine mixtures**: Stir melted chocolate mixture into the egg mixture, then fold in flour and salt.
5. **Fill ramekins**: Divide the batter among the ramekins and bake for 12-14 minutes until the edges are firm but the center is soft. Let cool for 1 minute before inverting onto plates.

Churro Bites with Chocolate Sauce

Ingredients:

For the Churros:

- 1 cup (240ml) water
- 1/2 cup (115g) unsalted butter
- 1 cup (125g) all-purpose flour
- 1/4 tsp salt
- 2 large eggs
- 1/4 cup (50g) granulated sugar
- 1 tsp ground cinnamon
- Oil for frying

For the Chocolate Sauce:

- 1/2 cup (120ml) heavy cream
- 1 cup (170g) semi-sweet chocolate chips

Instructions:

1. **Make dough**: In a saucepan, bring water and butter to a boil. Stir in flour and salt until combined. Remove from heat and let cool slightly.
2. **Add eggs**: Stir in eggs one at a time until smooth.
3. **Heat oil**: In a deep pot, heat oil to 350°F (175°C).
4. **Fry churros**: Pipe dough into hot oil and fry until golden brown, about 2-3 minutes. Drain on paper towels.
5. **Mix sugar and cinnamon**: In a bowl, combine sugar and cinnamon. Roll churros in the mixture while warm.
6. **Make chocolate sauce**: In a small saucepan, heat cream until simmering. Remove from heat and stir in chocolate chips until smooth. Serve churros with chocolate sauce.

Raspberry Lemon Bars

Ingredients:

For the Crust:

- 1 1/2 cups (190g) all-purpose flour
- 1/2 cup (100g) powdered sugar
- 1/2 cup (115g) unsalted butter, softened
- 1/4 tsp salt

For the Filling:

- 4 large eggs
- 1 cup (200g) granulated sugar
- 1/2 cup (120ml) freshly squeezed lemon juice
- 1 tbsp lemon zest
- 1/4 cup (30g) all-purpose flour
- 1 cup (150g) fresh raspberries

Instructions:

1. **Preheat oven**: Preheat your oven to 350°F (175°C) and grease a 9x9-inch baking dish.
2. **Make crust**: In a bowl, mix flour, powdered sugar, butter, and salt until crumbly. Press into the bottom of the baking dish.
3. **Bake crust**: Bake for 15-20 minutes until lightly golden.
4. **Prepare filling**: In another bowl, whisk together eggs, granulated sugar, lemon juice, lemon zest, and flour. Gently fold in raspberries.
5. **Fill crust**: Pour the filling over the baked crust.
6. **Bake**: Bake for an additional 20-25 minutes until set. Let cool before cutting into squares.

Chocolate-Covered Marshmallow Pops

Ingredients:

- 10 large marshmallows
- 1 cup (170g) semi-sweet chocolate chips
- 1 tbsp vegetable oil
- Sprinkles or crushed nuts (optional)
- Lollipop sticks

Instructions:

1. **Prepare marshmallows**: Insert lollipop sticks into each marshmallow.
2. **Melt chocolate**: In a microwave-safe bowl, melt chocolate chips and vegetable oil in 30-second intervals until smooth.
3. **Dip marshmallows**: Dip each marshmallow into the melted chocolate, allowing excess to drip off.
4. **Add toppings**: Roll in sprinkles or crushed nuts if desired.
5. **Set**: Place on a baking sheet lined with parchment paper and refrigerate until set.

Feel free to ask for more recipes or any adjustments!

Pineapple Upside-Down Cake

Ingredients:

- 1/4 cup (60g) unsalted butter
- 1/2 cup (100g) packed brown sugar
- 1 can (20 oz) sliced pineapple, drained
- Maraschino cherries (optional)
- 1 1/2 cups (190g) all-purpose flour
- 1 tsp baking powder
- 1/2 tsp baking soda
- 1/4 tsp salt
- 1/2 cup (100g) granulated sugar
- 1/4 cup (60ml) vegetable oil
- 1/2 cup (120ml) milk
- 1 tsp vanilla extract
- 2 large eggs

Instructions:

1. **Preheat oven**: Preheat your oven to 350°F (175°C).
2. **Prepare the topping**: In a 9-inch round cake pan, melt butter in the oven. Remove and sprinkle brown sugar evenly. Arrange pineapple slices and cherries on top.
3. **Mix dry ingredients**: In a bowl, whisk together flour, baking powder, baking soda, and salt.
4. **Combine wet ingredients**: In another bowl, beat granulated sugar, vegetable oil, milk, vanilla, and eggs until smooth.
5. **Combine mixtures**: Gradually add the dry ingredients to the wet mixture and mix until just combined.
6. **Pour batter**: Pour the batter over the pineapple layer in the pan.
7. **Bake**: Bake for 35-40 minutes or until a toothpick comes out clean. Let cool for 10 minutes, then invert onto a serving plate.

Almond Joy Fudge

Ingredients:

- 1 cup (170g) semi-sweet chocolate chips
- 1 can (14 oz) sweetened condensed milk
- 1/4 cup (60g) unsalted butter
- 1 cup (150g) shredded coconut
- 1/2 cup (75g) chopped almonds
- 1/2 cup (85g) milk chocolate chips

Instructions:

1. **Prepare the pan**: Line an 8x8-inch baking dish with parchment paper.
2. **Melt chocolate mixture**: In a saucepan over low heat, combine semi-sweet chocolate chips, sweetened condensed milk, and butter. Stir until melted and smooth.
3. **Spread base layer**: Pour half of the chocolate mixture into the prepared pan and spread evenly.
4. **Add coconut and almonds**: In a bowl, mix shredded coconut and chopped almonds. Spread the mixture over the chocolate layer in the pan.
5. **Add remaining chocolate**: Pour the remaining chocolate mixture on top and smooth it out.
6. **Chill**: Refrigerate for at least 2 hours until set. Cut into squares before serving.

Chocolate Hazelnut Tart

Ingredients:

For the Crust:

- 1 1/2 cups (190g) all-purpose flour
- 1/2 cup (50g) ground hazelnuts
- 1/4 cup (50g) powdered sugar
- 1/2 cup (115g) unsalted butter, softened
- 1 large egg yolk

For the Filling:

- 1 cup (240ml) heavy cream
- 8 oz (225g) dark chocolate, chopped
- 1/4 cup (60ml) hazelnut liqueur (optional)
- 1/2 cup (75g) chopped hazelnuts

Instructions:

1. **Preheat oven**: Preheat your oven to 350°F (175°C).
2. **Make crust**: In a bowl, mix flour, ground hazelnuts, and powdered sugar. Cut in butter until crumbly. Add egg yolk and mix until dough forms.
3. **Bake crust**: Press the dough into a tart pan and bake for 15-20 minutes until golden. Let cool.
4. **Prepare filling**: In a saucepan, heat heavy cream until simmering. Remove from heat and add chopped chocolate, stirring until melted and smooth. Stir in hazelnut liqueur if using.
5. **Fill tart**: Pour filling into the cooled crust and sprinkle chopped hazelnuts on top.
6. **Chill**: Refrigerate for at least 2 hours until set.

Maple Bacon Cupcakes

Ingredients:

For the Cupcakes:

- 1 cup (240ml) vegetable oil
- 1 cup (200g) granulated sugar
- 1/2 cup (100g) brown sugar
- 4 large eggs
- 1 cup (240ml) maple syrup
- 2 cups (250g) all-purpose flour
- 1 tsp baking powder
- 1/2 tsp baking soda
- 1/4 tsp salt
- 1 cup (150g) cooked bacon, chopped

For the Maple Frosting:

- 1 cup (230g) unsalted butter, softened
- 4 cups (480g) powdered sugar
- 1/4 cup (60ml) maple syrup
- 2-3 tbsp milk

Instructions:

1. **Preheat oven**: Preheat your oven to 350°F (175°C) and line a cupcake pan with liners.
2. **Mix wet ingredients**: In a bowl, mix vegetable oil, granulated sugar, brown sugar, eggs, and maple syrup until well combined.
3. **Combine dry ingredients**: In another bowl, whisk together flour, baking powder, baking soda, and salt. Gradually add to the wet mixture.
4. **Add bacon**: Fold in chopped bacon.
5. **Fill and bake**: Fill cupcake liners 2/3 full and bake for 18-20 minutes until a toothpick comes out clean. Let cool.
6. **Make frosting**: In a bowl, beat softened butter until creamy. Gradually add powdered sugar, maple syrup, and milk until desired consistency is reached.
7. **Frost cupcakes**: Frost cooled cupcakes and top with additional bacon bits if desired.

White Chocolate Raspberry Truffles

Ingredients:

- 8 oz (225g) white chocolate, chopped
- 1/2 cup (120ml) heavy cream
- 1/4 cup (60ml) raspberry puree (fresh or frozen)
- 1/4 cup (40g) crushed graham crackers or nuts for coating

Instructions:

1. **Melt chocolate**: In a saucepan, heat heavy cream until simmering. Pour over chopped white chocolate and let sit for 5 minutes. Stir until smooth.
2. **Add raspberry puree**: Stir in raspberry puree until well combined.
3. **Chill mixture**: Refrigerate for about 2 hours until firm.
4. **Form truffles**: Scoop out small amounts of the mixture and roll into balls.
5. **Coat truffles**: Roll truffles in crushed graham crackers or nuts.
6. **Chill again**: Place in the refrigerator until ready to serve.

Carrot Cake with Cream Cheese Frosting

Ingredients:

For the Cake:

- 2 cups (250g) all-purpose flour
- 2 cups (400g) granulated sugar
- 1 tsp baking powder
- 1 tsp baking soda
- 1/2 tsp salt
- 1 tsp ground cinnamon
- 1/2 tsp ground nutmeg
- 1 cup (240ml) vegetable oil
- 4 large eggs
- 3 cups (360g) grated carrots
- 1 cup (150g) crushed pineapple, drained
- 1/2 cup (80g) chopped walnuts (optional)

For the Frosting:

- 8 oz (225g) cream cheese, softened
- 1/2 cup (115g) unsalted butter, softened
- 4 cups (480g) powdered sugar
- 1 tsp vanilla extract

Instructions:

1. **Preheat oven:** Preheat your oven to 350°F (175°C) and grease two 9-inch round cake pans.
2. **Mix dry ingredients:** In a bowl, whisk together flour, sugar, baking powder, baking soda, salt, cinnamon, and nutmeg.
3. **Combine wet ingredients:** In another bowl, mix vegetable oil, eggs, grated carrots, and crushed pineapple.
4. **Combine mixtures:** Gradually add dry ingredients to the wet mixture and mix until just combined. Fold in chopped walnuts if using.
5. **Bake:** Divide batter between prepared pans and bake for 25-30 minutes until a toothpick comes out clean. Let cool.
6. **Make frosting:** In a bowl, beat cream cheese and butter until creamy. Gradually add powdered sugar and vanilla, mixing until smooth.

7. **Frost cake**: Once the cakes are cool, frost the top of one layer, place the second layer on top, and frost the top and sides.

Feel free to ask for more recipes or any adjustments!

www.ingramcontent.com/pod-product-compliance
Lightning Source LLC
LaVergne TN
LVHW081320060526
838201LV00055B/2378